CW00840633

UEFA
EURO 202
GERMANY

OFFICIAL
KIDS' GUIDE

WELBECK
CHILDREN'S BOOKS

Published under licence in 2024 by Welbeck Children's Books Limited
An imprint of the Hachette Children's Group

Welbeck Children's Books. An imprint of Hachette Children's Group
Part of Hodder & Stoughton Limited,Carmelite House,
50 Victoria Embankment, London EC4Y 0DZ
An Hachette Company
www.hachette.co.uk www.hachettechildrens.co.uk

ISBN 978 1 80453 590 5

10 9 8 7 6 5 4 3 2 1

Printed in Italy

Writer: Kevin Pettman
Senior commissioning editor: Suhel Ahmed
Design Manager: Sam James
Designer: Ben Ruocco
Consultant: Anthony Hobbs

The publishers would like to thank the following sources for their
kind permission to reproduce the pictures in this book.

All photography © Getty Images

The publisher has taken every reasonable step to ensure the accuracy of the facts
contained herein at the time of going to press, but can take no responsibility for any
incorrect information arising from changes that may take place after this point. For the
latest information, please visit: www.uefa.com/euro2024/

www.uefa.com constantly updates and maintains historical records pertaining
to the UEFA European Football Championship, and other UEFA competitions,
always aiming for 100% accuracy. Occasionally, however, new facts are brought
to light and they may have repercussions on the accuracy of the informations
here disclosed. Therefore, should you find any discrepencies in this information,
we would like to offer our apologies and we would welcome your comments.

The statistics and records in the book are correct as of January 2024.

A catalogue record for this book is available from the British Library.

CONTENTS

WELCOME TO UEFA EURO 2024

Europe's most exciting continental football competition gets under way this summer. UEFA (Union of European Football Associations) is the body in charge of football in Europe and organises the championship, which take place every four years.

On 14 June, hosts Germany get the championship under way in the opening game. Over the next four weeks the continent's best players will battle it out for the prize of being crowned EURO 2024 champions. Featuring 24 top nations and more than 500 players, the competition promises a footballing extravaganza for the supporters in the stadiums and the millions watching around the world.

Your Official EURO 2024 Kids' Guide has everything you need to know about the tournament, including an overview of the competition's history, fun facts and astounding stats, superstars to watch in 2024, a cool puzzles section, plus a results chart to fill in!

Kylian Mbappé scored twice in each of France's two qualifying matches against the Netherlands to secure his team's spot at EURO 2024.

THE SHOW KICKS OFF

The Munich Football Arena stages the opening match on Friday 14 June. As hosts, Germany feature in the first game and will be hoping to go all the way to the final in front of their home crowd! To get there, they will have to beat world-class teams packed with top talent. England, France and Portugal are just some of the other sides also chasing glory as they seek to lift the Henri Delaunay Cup this summer.

FACING THE BEST

The first UEFA European Championship took place in 1960 and featured only four teams in the final competition. Since EURO 2016, 24 sides have taken part in each edition. Apart from hosts Germany, the other 23 nations had to win their place at EURO 2024 through a series of tough qualifying games. After working so hard to qualify, no team wants to make an early exit from this famous competition!

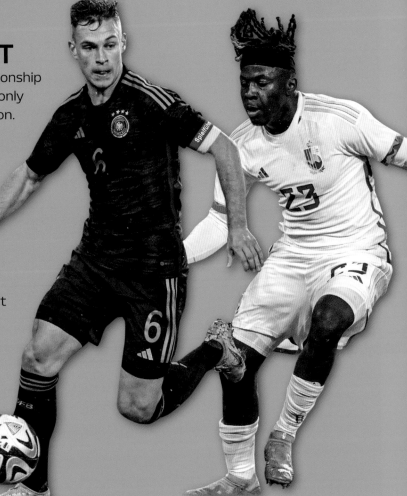

Germany's Joshua Kimmich (l) is currently regarded as one of the best midfielders in the world.

REIGNING CHAMPIONS

Italy were the proud winners of EURO 2020, which took place in 2021 as a result of the COVID pandemic. The *Azzurri,* as Italy are nicknamed, defeated England in the final after a dramatic penalty shoot-out. EURO 2020 is also remembered for staging the matches in some of the great European stadiums spanning 11 different countries. It was as part of the 60th anniversary celebrations of the iconic tournament.

Since 1960, every winner of the championship has lifted the Henri Delaunay Cup. The trophy is named in honour of UEFA's first general secretary.

Italy midfielder Jorginho hugs the trophy after his side beat England in the final of UEFA EURO 2020.

HOW THE FINALS WORK

With 51 matches scheduled during a mega month of international football, you're guaranteed to see plenty of action from the first kick-off to the moment the winning captain lifts the trophy.

GROUP DRAMA

On 2 December 2023, the teams that had qualified were drawn into six groups of four, lettered A to F. Before the draw, Germany already knew they would be in Group A. In the finals, each team plays the three others in their group. Once the games are concluded, the top two from each group, plus the four best third-placed nations, go through to the round of 16. The drama in this group stage is intense as teams chase points.

Rodri of Spain battles for the ball against Sweden's Alexander Isak at UEFA EURO 2020.

ROUND OF 16

The round of 16 begins the knockout phase and dials up the tension and drama. The opponents each of the 16 teams play depends on their final position in the groups (see pages 58-59). From this round onwards, games tied after 90 minutes play extra time and if that fails to separate the two teams, a nail-biting penalty shoot-out decides who goes through. The eight winners march on to the quarter-finals and the losers exit the tournament.

EURO 2020 saw 94 goals scored in the group stage. Will EURO 2024 beat that?

QUARTER-FINALS

The four quarter-final matches are on 5 and 6 July at venues in Stuttgart, Hamburg, Berlin and Düsseldorf. With a place in the final four at stake, this is where teams begin to believe they could go all the way. A solid defence is vital but teams must take their chances to grab the win. At EURO 2020, England cruised past Ukraine 4-0 in their quarter-final clash!

SEMI-FINALS

In the compeitition's recent past, players such as Harry Kane, Cristiano Ronaldo and Antoine Griezmann have been heroic goalscorers for their country in semi-finals. This year, who will be hitting the net and helping their side secure a place in the final? The first semi-final is on 9 July in Munich with the second scheduled for the following day in Dortmund.

England's Bukayo Saka was one of the young stars who shone at EURO 2020.

THE FINAL

The final game of EURO 2024 takes place on 14 July in Berlin. For both finalists it will be their seventh fixture of the tournament, with 90 minutes separating them from realising their football dream. Having said that, the EURO 2020 final went to a penalty shoot-out, so be prepared for 30 minutes extra and even dramatic spot kicks to decide the champions!

Italy held their nerve to win the penalty shoot-out 3-2 against England in the EURO 2020 final.

MEET THE HOSTS

Winners of three UEFA European Championship titles (as West Germany in 1972 and 1980 and a unified Germany in 1996), the hosts are a powerhouse in world football. Germany also have four FIFA World Cup crowns. UEFA EURO 2024 is the 14th time they have played at the finals and it is the second time they are hosting the tournament*. The first was in 1988, when they lost to the Netherlands in the semi-final.

CITY GUIDE

Ten cities will be inviting the 24 teams and travelling fans this summer. From Hamburg in the north to Stuttgart and Munich in the south, with Berlin, Gelsenkirchen, Dortmund, Düsseldorf, Leipzig, Cologne and Frankfurt in between, Germany is ready to put on a football party to remember. Having hosted four matches during EURO 2020, Germany has the distinction of being the first country to stage European Championship games in consecutive tournaments.

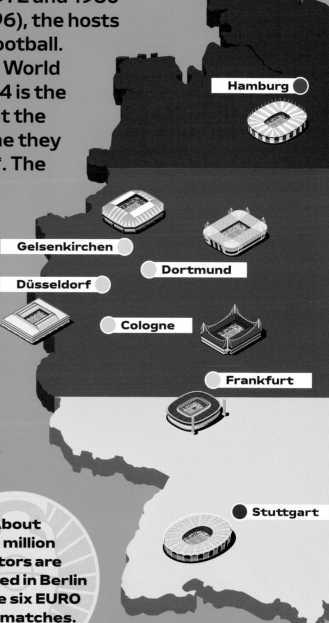

Hamburg

Gelsenkirchen

Dortmund

Düsseldorf

Cologne

Frankfurt

Stuttgart

About 2.5 million visitors are expected in Berlin for the six EURO 2024 matches.

FOOTBALL FANATICS

Football is the national sport in Germany. The nation has produced winning international teams in both the men's and women's game, plus its top-tier domestic league competition, the Bundesliga, features world-famous clubs such as Bayern Munich and Borussia Dortmund. The atmosphere generated at German stadiums is electric, and this will be amped up even more when EURO 2024 kicks off.

HOME ADVANTAGE

The last two showpiece finals were staged in London (EURO 2020) and Paris (EURO 2016). Hosts England reached the final of EURO 2020, while France as hosts made the 2016 final. Can Germany make home advantage count too and go all the way to the final? History is on their side. At the 1974 FIFA World Cup, Germany were hosts and lifted the trophy. Now, 50 years on, the stage is set for them to repeat the feat at this championship.

● Berlin

○ Leipzig

● Munich

*Excludes Germany's involvement in jointly hosting EURO 2020.

STADIUM SPOTLIGHT

Check out the ten stunning stadiums staging UEFA EURO 2024 games this summer.

OLYMPIASTADION

City: **Berlin**
Capacity: **71,000**
UEFA EURO 2024 matches:
**3 x Group stage, 1 x Round of 16,
1 x Quarter-final, Final**
As the tournament's largest venue, the Olympiastadion Berlin is a fitting setting to crown the new European champions on 14 July. The venue is no stranger to the big occasion, having hosted the 2006 FIFA World Cup final and the 2015 UEFA Champions League final.

COLOGNE STADIUM

City: **Cologne**
Capacity: 43,000
UEFA EURO 2024 matches:
4 x Group stage, 1 x Round of 16
Home to Bundesliga side FC Köln, Cologne Stadium is gearing up for the first of its four group games on 15 June. It was reconstructed for the 2006 FIFA World Cup and also staged the final of the UEFA Europa League in 2020.

DÜSSELDORF ARENA

City: **Düsseldorf**
Capacity: **47,000**
UEFA EURO 2024 matches: **3 x Group stage, 1 x Round of 16, 1 x Quarter-final**
Düsseldorf hosts its first EURO 2024 action on 17 June. The stadium's fabulous acoustics will impress the 40,000+ fans who will be packed inside this vibrant ground. It might be one of the smaller stadiums but is known for generating a 'party-like' atmosphere.

BVB STADION DORTMUND

City: **Dortmund**
Capacity: **62,000**
UEFA EURO 2024 matches:
4 x Group stage, 1 x Round of 16, 1 x Semi-final
Spectators coming to this iconic stadium are in for a treat. The home of German giants Borussia Dortmund, the venue's most famous feature is the huge 'Yellow Wall' stand that evokes such passion among supporters.

FRANKFURT ARENA

City: **Frankfurt**
Capacity: **47,000**
UEFA EURO 2024 matches:
4 x Group stage , 1 x Round of 16
Originally built in 1925, the Frankfurt Arena has undergone several updates since and is a superb football venue with centrally placed screens over the turf. The ground gets its first taste of UEFA EURO 2024 on 17 June. Previously it has staged matches at the 2006 FIFA World Cup and the FIFA Women's World Cup final in 2011.

ARENA AUFSCHALKE

City: **Gelsenkirchen**
Capacity: **50,000**
UEFA EURO 2024 matches:
3 x Group stage, 1 x Round of 16
Opened in 2001, this marvellous stadium boasts a retractable roof and a slide-out pitch. A modern construction but with a traditional feel, Arena AufSchalke will be a big hit with supporters who have tickets for the matches at this venue.

VOLKSPARKSTADION

City: **Hamburg**
Capacity: **49,000**
UEFA EURO 2024 matches:
4 x Group stage, 1 x Quarter-final
The Volksparkstadion welcomes European Championship football again, 36 years after it did so in 1988. A significant upgrade in 2000 has turned this into a state-of-the-art footballing venue and the design ensures superb views from every seat.

LEIPZIG STADIUM

City: **Leipzig**
Capacity: **40,000**
UEFA EURO 2024 matches: **3 x Group stage, 1 x Round of 16**

This charming ground mixes the old with the new. The fascinating venue features a stunning roof that was unveiled in 2004, but in a homage to the past, the construction was built inside the shell of the old Zentralstadion, which was the biggest stadium in the former East Germany.

MUNICH FOOTBALL ARENA

City: **Munich**
Capacity: **66,000**
UEFA EURO 2024 matches:
4 x Group stage, 1 x Round of 16, 1 x Semi-final

Munich is where the EURO party gets under way! A packed Munich Football Arena will be pulsating for the opening match. Bayern Munich play their home games here, so players such as Leon Goretzka and Jamal Musiala are sure to get a huge reception from the fans.

STUTTGART ARENA

City: **Stuttgart**
Capacity: **51,000**
UEFA EURO 2024 matches:
4 x Group stage, 1 x Quarter-final

The original stadium was built in 1933, but revamps and modern additions have turned it into an awe-inspiring venue for watching live football. What's more, with its famous museums and scenic views, Stuttgart is a great city to enjoy the tournament.

GRAND FINALS

Ten nations have been lucky enough to become European champions. Here's a reminder of some of the competition's most memorable finals.

UEFA EURO 2020*

Champions: **Italy**

Runners-up: **England**

Italy and England were the tournament's standout teams, with strong defences and creative forward lines. In the final, England netted after just two minutes, but Italy equalised mid-way through the second half and the score remained 1-1 even after extra time. A nail-biting shoot-out saw Italy triumph 3-2 on penalties and the drama capped a wonderful competition!

*Held in 2021 due to the Covid pandemic

UEFA EURO 2016

Champions: **Portugal**

Runners-up: **France**

With the showpiece game taking place in Paris, France were the favourites to win their third European Championship. A tight and tense game saw Portugal captain Cristiano Ronaldo leave the pitch injured in the first half, but his team-mates showed their quality. Eder's superb strike in extra time broke the deadlock and Portugal held on to win their first major trophy.

UEFA EURO 2012

Champions: **Spain** | Runners-up: **Italy**

Spain's 4-0 victory over Italy was the highest winning margin in the final of this famous event. Fernando Torres was among the scorers, who also netted the winner in the EURO 2008 final to become the first player to score in two European Championship finals.

> **The last single host nation to win the European Championship was France in 1984.**

UEFA EURO 2000

Champions: **France** | Runners-up: **Italy**

Italy were heading for a 1-0 victory until France's Sylvain Wiltord swept the ball home in the fourth minute of stoppage time to take the match into extra time. In the 103rd minute, David Trezeguet scored an extra-time golden goal to capture the EURO crown for France. Probably the most dramatic final ever!

UEFA EURO 1992

Champions: **Denmark**
Runners-up: **Germany**

Denmark were crowned kings of Europe 32 years ago after their stunning victory over giants Germany. They were late entrants into the competition, but with Peter Schmeichel, John Jensen and Brian Laudrup in their line-up, they played with style and confidence. They beat Germany 2-0 in a classic final in Gothenburg.

EURO FINALS SCORES

1960	USSR 2-1 Yugoslavia
1964	Spain 2-1 USSR
1968	Italy 2-0 Yugoslavia*
1972	West Germany 3-0 USSR
1976	Czechoslovakia 2-2 West Germany**
1980	West Germany 2-1 Belgium
1984	France 2-0 Spain
1988	Netherlands 2-0 USSR
1992	Denmark 2-0 Germany
1996	Germany 2-1 Czech Republic
2000	France 2-1 Italy
2004	Greece 1-0 Portugal
2008	Spain 1-0 Germany
2012	Spain 4-0 Italy
2016	Portugal 1-0 France
2020	Italy 1-1 England***

*Italy won replay after 1-1 draw.
**Czechoslovakia won on penalties.
***Italy won on penalties.

UEFA EURO 1988

Champions: **Netherlands**
Runners-up: **USSR**

The one thing fans remember from the 1988 final is Marco van Basten's blistering volleyed goal! The strike gave the Netherlands a 2-0 lead, which was the final score as the Dutch claimed their first major international prize. Ruud Gullit, Ronald Koeman and Frank Rijkaard were three other world-class Dutch stars in the team.

With five goals, the Netherlands' Marco van Basten was top scorer at the 1988 finals.

PERSONAL PRIZES

As well as the Henri Delaunay Cup, players can pick up personal prizes during EURO 2024. While team-work is essential for success, individual brilliance can often decide the outcome of a match and lead to an awesome award too. Check out what's on offer.

SHARP SHOOTER

The tournament's top forwards will be chasing the Top Scorer award for netting the most goals during the competition. With a rich history from past tournaments, one super striker will be looking to add his name to the record books. At EURO 2020, Portugal's Cristiano Ronaldo bagged five goals to win it. And at EURO 2016, France's Antoine Griezmann won the award with his six strikes.

YOUNG AWARD

Players born on or after 1 January 2002 will be in the running to be named the UEFA EURO 2024 Young Player of the Tournament. They will need to catch the eye of the Technical Observer team, with their skill, game impact and ability to handle the big stage. Spain midfielder Pedri (right), at 18 years old, took this special award at EURO 2020.

France's Michel Platini scored a record nine goals at the European Championship in 1984.

Italy's keeper Gianluigi Donnarumma made many heroic saves to help his team triumph at EURO 2020.

TOP PLAYERS

The trophy awarding does not stop there. After each contest, a Player of the Match is selected and a trophy is handed to the game's top performer. Luka Modrić (Croatia), Kevin De Bruyne (Belgium) and Bukayo Saka (England) were among prize winners at UEFA EURO 2020, and were all named in the Team of the Tournament. Get ready to see players impress at EURO 2024.

SHINING STAR

UEFA's team of Technical Observers have the tough task of choosing a Player of the Tournament. These experts look at how well players have performed and their impact on results. At EURO 2020, Italy goalkeeper Gianluigi Donnarumma was picked as the tournament's shining star. Antoine Griezmann (France), Andrés Iniesta (Spain) and Theodoros Zagorakis (Greece) are others who have been chosen in the past.

Lively Lukaku

Romelu Lukaku, Belgium's all-time top scorer, was named Player of the Match for his nation's first two UEFA EURO 2020 games.

CHAMPIONSHIP RECORD BREAKERS

Let's turn the clock back and look at the nations and players who have made it into the record books of this iconic competition.

WONDROUS WINNERS

UEFA EURO 2024 hosts Germany have played a record 53 games at the European Championships, winning 27 and scoring 78 goals. They are also three-time champions, a record they jointly hold with Spain.

GOALS GALORE

EURO 2020 saw the most goals netted at a European Championship. In total, 142 strikes were scored, beating the previous best of 108 set at the 2016 edition.

FASTEST FINAL GOAL

England left-back Luke Shaw (right) created history at the EURO 2020 final by scoring after just one minute and 56 seconds. It is the fastest goal ever scored in the competition's showpiece game.

FINAL FLOURISH

Italy defender Leonardo Bonucci claims the record as the oldest player to score in a EURO final. He netted a goal in the same game as Shaw (above), aged 34 years and 71 days.

DUTCH DELIGHT

Across all 16 editions of the European Championship, only the Netherlands have scored six goals during a match. It came during their 6–1 win against Yugoslavia at EURO 2000.

OWN NO!

An unwanted record was created at EURO 2020 with 11 own goals scored in the competition. This was two more than the nine scored in all the previous tournaments combined!

Spain's keeper Unai Simón is unhappy after letting in Pedri's back pass at EURO 2020.

HAT-TRICK HEROES

Eight players have scored a hat-trick at a European Championship. Spain's David Silva (below) was the last, at EURO 2008. France playmaker Michel Platini is the only player to score two hat-tricks, both in the 1984 edition.

FATHER'S FOOTSTEPS

When Italy's Federico Chiesa (above) scored at EURO 2020, he followed the achievement of his father, Enrico, who had netted at EURO 1996. They are the only father and son duo to score at the tournament.

SHUT OUT

Legendary Spain goalkeeper Iker Casillas boasts the best clean sheet record. Across appearances at EURO 2004, 2008 and 2012 he totalled nine games where he did not let in a goal.

PICK OF THE COACHES

Although it is the players who win matches, the coach is just as important. The coach is responsible for the training, tactics and selection, and for guiding the team to victory.

PREP TIME

Before the team takes to the pitch on matchday, the coach and their staff train the players. The coach makes sure the players are match fit, understand their role in the team and the strategies they will use to beat their opponents. Preparation begins weeks before the competition kicks off and continues throughout the tournament.

SQUAD SELECTION

The coach has the final say over which players are selected for the squad and the ones who make it on the team sheet on matchday. He will assess the strengths and qualities they add, either as a starting option or an impact substitute from the bench. The best coaches build great bonds with their players and inspire them to perform at their very best.

TALKING TACTICS

A key part of the coach's role is deciding how the team will play. Often called the tactics, this determines whether the style is defensive, where the team soaks up pressure and looks either to counter attack or score from a set piece, or attacking. In an attacking system, a coach may play with several forwards and hope to break down the opponent's defence, and score as many goals as possible.

Coach Roberto Mancini guided Italy to EURO 2020 triumph.

ROBERTO MARTÍNEZ

Team: **Portugal**

This is Martínez's first tournament as Portugal coach, having previously been in charge of Belgium between 2016 and 2022. Portugal are historically coached to press opponents high up the pitch, and it will be interesting to see how Martínez sets up the young side to play around the talismanic Cristiano Ronaldo.

DIDIER DESCHAMPS

Team: **France**

Deschamps has Kylian Mbappé – among the world's best forwards – in his team. He has a system where Mbappé can flourish and link with a central striker, as well as receive decisive passes from attack-minded midfielders. Deschamps coached France to second place at UEFA EURO 2016.

LUIS DE LA FUENTE

Team: **Spain**

Appointed coach of a talented squad in 2022, he guided Spain to the UEFA Nations League title after just six months. De la Fuente likes his team to control possession, be confident in passing and use space on the wings for Spain's skilled wingers and full-backs to launch attacks.

GARETH SOUTHGATE

Team: **England**

Southgate has been in charge since 2016, guiding England to the final at UEFA EURO 2020. With the backbone of that team still involved, they have experience of winning tournament games. Southgate's team plays the ball out from defence, with creative midfielders such as Jude Bellingham and Declan Rice feeding their leading striker Harry Kane.

PLAYERS TO WATCH:
FORWARDS

It's time to take a closer look at some of the stars of UEFA EURO 2024. First up are some of the competition's finest forwards, so check out their goal scoring skills and qualities on the pitch.

KYLIAN MBAPPÉ

Country: **France**
Club: **Paris Saint-Germain**
Born: **20 December 1998**
Major honours: **FIFA World Cup 2018, UEFA Nations League 2021, Ligue 1 (x6)**

Named France captain in 2023, Mbappé is undoubtedly one of the world's top strikers with a mix of speed, skills and sharp shooting in attack. He netted 40 goals in his first 70 international appearances and gives defenders nightmares thanks to his lethal finishing. This fearsome forward could shoot France to glory in Germany.

HARRY KANE

Country: **England**
Club: **Bayern Munich**
Born: **28 July 1993**
Major honours: **UEFA EURO 2020 runner-up, FIFA World Cup 2018 fourth place**

Kane has come close before in international tournaments, most noticeably when England lost the UEFA EURO 2020 final on penalties. He is his country's record scorer and whether striking inside the box or linking play in deeper areas, Kane's influence is immense. He is an expert penalty taker and the player England turn to whenever a goal is needed.

ÁLVARO MORATA

Country: **Spain**
Club: **Atlético de Madrid**
Born: **23 October 1992**
Major honours: **UEFA Nations League 2023, UEFA Champions League (x2), La Liga (x2), Serie A (x2)**

With six goals across EURO 2016 and EURO 2020, Morata is Spain's highest goalscorer at the tournament. Tall, powerful and clinical with his feet and in the air, the striker adds experience to complement Spain's youthful midfielders and attackers around him. His return of 34 goals in 68 games proves what a potent force he is up front.

RASMUS HØJLUND

Country: **Denmark**
Club: **Manchester United**
Born: **4 February 2003**
Major honours: **none to date**

Denmark's star striker has been on a goal blitz since netting a hat-trick on his first international start in March 2023. That was against Finland in a UEFA EURO 2024 qualifier and he boosted his stats further to register six goals from his opening four qualifying games. The youngster has the movement, skill and natural goal-scoring instinct needed by all top strikers.

SERGE GNABRY

Country: **Germany**
Club: **Bayern Munich**
Born: **14 July 1995**
Major honours: **UEFA Champions League (x1) , FIFA Club World Cup (x1), Bundesliga (x5)**

Gnabry celebrates his birthday on 14 July — the UEFA EURO 2024 final day. There is a good chance his goals, assists and smart forward play can take Germany all the way this summer. What a birthday celebration that would be?! Gnabry has the intelligence to play in a range of attacking positions and the coolness to convert chances inside the box.

CRISTIANO RONALDO

Country: **Portugal**
Club: **Al Nassr**
Born: **5 February 1985**
Major honours: **UEFA EURO 2016,
UEFA Nations League 2019,
UEFA Champions League (x5)**

Even at 39, Ronaldo is still an amazing forward who can ignite a match with a moment of pure magic. With more than 120 international goals and having broken the 200-appearance mark in 2023, Ronaldo could still use all his striking prowess, experience and leadership skills to push his team to victory. The signs are good; he scored five in his opening four EURO 2024 qualifiers.

ROMELU LUKAKU

Country: **Belgium**
Club: **Roma (on loan)**
Born: **13 May 1993**
Major honours: **Serie A (x1)**

Lukaku is a menace to defend against because his physical presence, smart footwork and laser-guided shooting create so many opportunities. The striker has proved his pedigree in major tournaments, netting both at EURO 2020 and EURO 2016. With 79 goals in 112 appearances to date, he is Belgium's star man in attack.

ALEKSANDAR MITROVIĆ

Country: **Serbia**
Club: **Al-Hilal**
Born: **16 September 1994**
Major honours: **Belgian Pro League (x1), Serbian SuperLiga (x1)**

Boasting an incredible 57 goals in 85 internationals, Mitrović revels in playing for his country and leads the frontline with power and fantastic all-round vision. He works hard inside and outside the box, using good acceleration to beat defenders and timing his runs perfectly to convert crosses. Mitrović will be a big threat at his first European Championships.

ANTOINE GRIEZMANN

Country: **France**
Club: **Atlético de Madrid**
Born: **21 March 1991**
Major honours: **FIFA World Cup 2018, UEFA Nations League 2021, UEFA Europa League 2018**

Griezmann has always been a potent part of France's firepower alongside Mbappé, shooting 44 goals in 125 outings. What's more, his creative skills now add another dimension to his play. The forward can drop deep to build play, drift wide to stretch defences and glide past opponents with ease. France is lucky to have this talismanic figure.

MEMPHIS DEPAY

Country: **Netherlands**
Club: **Atlético de Madrid**
Born: **13 February 1994**
Major honours: **FIFA World Cup 2014 third place, La Liga (x1), Eredivisie (x1)**

Over the years Depay has developed from a lively winger into a world-class centre forward with the ability to score from any angle or opportunity. Fast and very alert inside the final third, Depay's record of 44 goals in 88 international games demonstrates his effectiveness at this level. He links very well with a striking partner and can play in a range of systems.

PLAYERS TO WATCH:
MIDFIELDERS

Midfielders play a crucial role, joining defence with attack and covering huge distances to dictate the style of play. These players need skill, energy and great passing abilities.

JAMAL MUSIALA

Country: **Germany**
Club: **Bayern Munich**
Born: **26 February 2003**
Major honours **Bundesliga (x4), UEFA Super Cup (x1), FIFA Club World Cup (x1)**

Any teenager selected to play for Germany has to be a special talent – and that is exactly what Musiala is! A versatile, technically gifted and visionary attacker, he can play across the midfield positions and operate between the lines to great effect. He burst onto the international scene three years ago, making an impression at EURO 2020.

PEDRI

Country: **Spain**
Club: **Barcelona**
Born: **25 November 2002**
Major honours: **La Liga (x1)**

Along with Barcelona team-mate Gavi, Pedri represents a talented new generation looking to emulate the previous Spain triumphs of 1964, 2008 and 2012. Pedri is a world-class attacking midfielder thanks to his close control, mobility, tactical awareness and ability to launch quick and precise forward moves. Recipient of the EURO 2020 Young Player of the Tournament, Pedri is key to Spain's success this summer.

JORGINHO

Country: **Italy**
Club: **Arsenal**
Born: **20 December 1991**
Major honours:
UEFA EURO 2020, UEFA Champions League (x1), UEFA Europa League (x1)

There are few players like Jorginho. The experienced central midfielder performs as a fantastic pivot for Italy, accepting the ball in tight spaces and being able to turn and pick a telling forward pass. He knows how to pressure opponents and pounce on mistakes, plus his penalty technique is one of the finest at EURO 2024.

BUKAYO SAKA

Country: **England**
Club: **Arsenal**
Born: **5 September 2001**
Major honours: **UEFA EURO 2020 runner-up, UEFA Europa League runner-up (x1)**

As a teenager, Saka announced himself at EURO 2020 – his first senior international event. After a stellar qualifying campaign for this tournament, where Saka excelled in support of stars like Harry Kane and Marcus Rashford, he is ready to impress again. In wide areas he has a devastating mix of dribbling, speed and passing skills and regularly chips in with goals.

LUKA MODRIĆ

Country: **Croatia**
Club: **Real Madrid**
Born: **9 September 1985**
Major honours: **FIFA World Cup 2018 runner-up, UEFA Nations League 2023 runner-up, UEFA Champions League (x5)**

Modrić's career with Croatia goes back to 2006 and over those 18 years he has dazzled for both club and country. Able to operate as a playmaker or even a defensively-minded central midfielder, Modrić exerts such an influence on the pitch and can control the tempo of a game. His touch, passing range, energy and leadership are key to Croatia's success.

AURÉLIEN TCHOUAMÉNI

Country: **France**
Club: **Real Madrid**
Born: **27 January 2000**
Major honours: **UEFA Nations League 2021, FIFA World Cup 2022 runner-up**

Although France boast an awesome attack, the frontline is supported by an equally formidable midfield. In particular, they have one of Europe's top defensive midfielders in Tchouaméni to keep them tough at the back! This is the Real Madrid star's first European Championship, and his tackling, clearances, blocks and passing are key if France are to reach yet another final.

DUŠAN TADIĆ

Country: **Serbia**
Club: **Fenerbahçe SK**
Born: **20 November 1988**
Major honours: **Eredivisie (x3)**

The Serbia captain contributes in so many ways to the team's play. Tadić is a wonderful passer, can finish chances inside the box and is an expert at set pieces. He always stays calm under pressure and his creativity makes him adept at finding a way to unlock defences. Watch Tadić drift into spaces where opponents struggle to pick him up.

BRUNO FERNANDES

Country: **Portugal**
Club: **Manchester United**
Born: **8 September 1994**
Major honours: **UEFA Nations League 2019, UEFA Europa League runner-up (x1)**

Fernandes contributed two assists and one goal as Portugal won their first four EURO 2024 qualifiers to set their sights on the finals in Germany. He enjoys a lot of possession and strives to take the ball in midfield areas and release a forward with an accurate pass. With Cristiano Ronaldo, Rafeal Leão and Bernardo Silva around him, Fernandes is able to orchestrate attack after attack.

DOMINIK SZOBOSZLAI

Country: **Hungary**
Club: **Liverpool**
Born: **25 October 2000**
Major honours: **Austrian Bundesliga (x4)**

Szoboszlai has quickly become a central figure for Hungary and a worthy recipient of the captain's armband. He scored the play-off winning goal to send Hungary to EURO 2020 but could not play at the finals because of injury. This tournament will showcase his individual skill, brilliant free-kick technique and all-round midfield qualities which shine on the international stage.

KEVIN DE BRUYNE

Country: **Belgium**
Club: **Manchester City**
Born: **28 June 1991**
Major honours: **UEFA Champions League (x1), Premier League (x5)**

Blessed with talents few can match, De Bruyne can control a game with his passing and movement from central midfield. The playmaker will spray a long ball straight to a team-mate's boot or play into space for a winger or forward to collect. He covers so much of the pitch and his set piece delivery is a joy for Belgium's attack line. This is De Bruyne's third European Championships.

ACTIVITY ZONE

Welcome to the UEFA EURO 2024 Official Kids' Guide puzzle section! Get ready to test your football knowledge to the maximum. Good luck.

TOP TENS

Here are ten players who have worn number ten for their country at a past European Championship. Fill in the missing letters from each name.

1. ZI☐☐NE

2. XH☐K☐

3. ROO☐☐Y

4. HA☐A☐D

5. D☐☐AY

6. MOD☐☐Ć

7. C☐S☐A

8. ☐ÀBRE☐☐S

9. POD☐☐SKI

10. IB☐☐HIMOV☐Ć

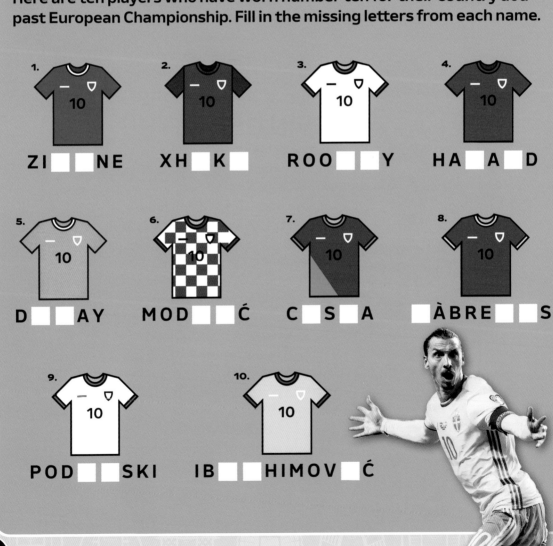

TEN TESTS

Tick if you think the statement is true or false.

	True	False
1. Cristiano Ronaldo scored 10 goals at EURO 2020.	◯	◯
2. There were a record 10 red cards at EURO 2000.	◯	◯
3. England hosted EURO 1996 – the 10th edition of the cup.	◯	◯
4. The EURO 2016 final match in Paris kicked off at 10:10pm local time.	◯	◯
5. Counting West Germany and Germany together, nine other nations (making a total of 10) have won the European Championship.	◯	◯
6. Ten penalties were taken in the shoot-out to decide the EURO 2020 final.	◯	◯
7. Denmark have won 10 games in total at the European Championships.	◯	◯
8. Ten cities across Europe hosted EURO 2020 matches.	◯	◯
9. Ten goals were scored in the EURO 2012 final between Spain and Italy.	◯	◯
10. Italy have appeared at 10 European Championships.	◯	◯

Answers on page 64.

SPOT THE DIFFERENCE

Here is an action shot from a European Qualifiers match between Scotland and Spain in 2023. The image below it may seem identical but has six differences – can you circle them all?

PAY THE PENALTY

A penalty is being taken in each of these UEFA EURO 2024 qualifying games. Extra balls have been added, but which is the real ball in each?

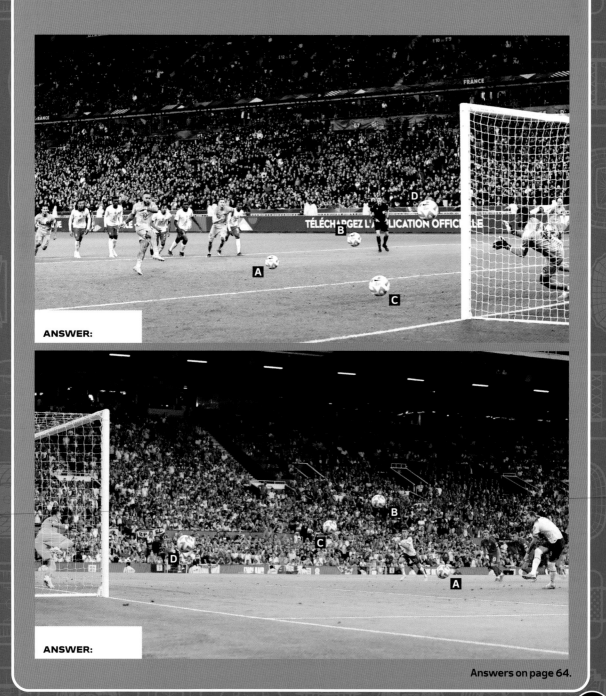

ANSWER:

ANSWER:

Answers on page 64.

KIT CLOSE-UP

The camera has zoomed in on these shirts worn during UEFA EURO 2024 qualifiers. Which national team does each belong to?

1.

2.

3.

4.

5.

6.

TRAIN GAME

These three EURO stars are pictured in training gear and not their usual match shirts. Can you work out who they are?

A

B

C

Answers on page 64.

GOAL COUNT

Legendary players have scored lots of goals at EURO finals over the years. Can you match each forward with their total goal count?

7   6   14   5   4   9

Patrick Kluivert (Netherlands) ☐

Antoine Griezmann (France) ☐

David Villa (Spain) ☐

Michel Platini (France) ☐

Cristiano Ronaldo (Portugal) ☐

Marco van Basten (Netherlands) ☐

GOAL SCRAMBLE

Can you unscramble the names of these ace goalscorers? They all netted during UEFA EURO 2024 qualifying.

1. KAYAK BOA US

2. JAM UNSOLD RUSH

3. MAC COTTON MISTY

4. BELOWS NETWORK RAID

5. FEAR ÃLOE LA

6. HANDING EAR ALL

Answers on page 64.

EURO NUMBER CODE

The numbers below represent the equivalent letter in the alphabet, so 1 = A, 2 = B, 3 = C all the way to 26 = Z. Study the numbers here to reveal three countries that are playing at UEFA EURO 2024.

1.

7	5	18	13	1	14	25

2.

16	15	18	20	21	7	1	12

3.

19	3	15	20	12	1	14	4

PICK THE DIGITS

The answer to each of these questions has either a 9, 1, 0, 4 or 6 in it, or any combination of the numbers. Pick the digits you think are correct, and remember that they can be used more than once.

A. The year Spain first won the trophy:

☐ ☐ ☐ ☐

B. The age of Cristiano Ronaldo when he scored at EURO 2004:

☐ ☐

C. The height, in centimetres, of the Henri Delaunay Cup:

☐ ☐

D. The height, in centimetres, of Italy's star EURO 2020 goalkeeper Gianluigi Donnarumma (right):

☐ ☐ ☐

E. The shirt number Germany star Jamal Musiala wore at EURO 2020:

☐ ☐

Answers on page 64.

CHAMPIONS SEARCH

Can you find all 15 European champions in this grid?

U	L	V	X	J	V	I	E	I	R	A	T	Z	G
W	F	D	O	S	O	C	A	S	I	L	L	A	S
O	S	Y	R	C	N	R	O	U	Q	J	X	G	F
N	W	M	U	G	X	K	G	C	C	G	V	O	C
T	A	L	O	N	S	O	Q	I	L	T	N	R	H
E	V	D	A	E	H	Y	S	K	N	I	E	A	I
C	C	E	E	X	S	I	L	V	A	H	C	K	E
T	A	X	R	S	U	K	K	G	J	F	O	I	L
S	X	R	I	R	C	P	D	M	U	V	L	S	L
H	E	I	V	X	A	H	E	Y	E	L	C	L	I
Q	S	N	B	A	U	T	A	P	W	D	L	T	N
C	B	J	K	S	L	K	T	M	E	M	E	I	I
I	J	K	P	H	D	H	X	I	P	D	H	R	T
X	A	V	I	R	A	M	O	S	L	S	V	R	P

ALONSO	EDER	SILVA
CARVALHO	GULLIT	VERRATTI
CASILLAS	JORGINHO	VIEIRA
CHIELLINI	PEPE	XAVI
DESCHAMPS	RAMOS	ZAGORAKIS

WORD FIT

Use the football clues below to fill in the answers. Some letters have been added to help you.

ACROSS
1. This German city will host the UEFA EURO 2024 opening game.
2. The Video Assistant Referee is better known as this.
3. In this position, the player's main job is to stop the opposition scoring.
4. Nickname of the England team.
5. If a player gets this card, he must leave the game.

DOWN
6. The name of the move in which a player kicks the ball between the legs of an opposing player.
7. This type of goal can be scored when the ball is in the air.
8. This person is in charge of a game.
9. This nation is famous for its orange kit.

Answers on page 64.

HIT OR MISS?

Look at the photos from UEFA EURO 2020 and in each instance decide whether the player scored or missed with their shot.

ROMELU LUKAKU,
Finland v Belgium

Hit   Miss
○   ○

RAHEEM STERLING,
Czech Republic v England

Hit   Miss
○   ○

DIOGO JOTA,
Portugal v Germany

Hit   Miss

ÁLVARO MORATA,
Spain v Poland

Hit   Miss

IVAN PERIŠIĆ,
Croatia v Czech Republic

Hit   Miss

KAI HAVERTZ,
Portugal v Germany

Hit   Miss

Answers on page 64.

YEAR WE GO

Here is a stack of questions with a year as the answer. Good luck knowing these important dates!

FLASHBACK

Here are pictures of Cristiano Ronaldo at UEFA EURO 2004, 2008, 2012, 2016 and 2020. Write the correct year under each action shot.

1.

2.

3.

4.

5.

HOST PARTY

Do you know when these countries were the sole hosts of a UEFA EURO tournament? Draw arrows from each country to the correct year.

 FRANCE    SWEDEN    ITALY

1980   2016   1992

BIRTHDAYS BOYS

These players were all born in the same year, but what was it?

Jordan Pickford
England

Memphis Depay
Netherlands

Emre Can
Germany

Leandro Trossard
Belgium

The year is:

DEBUT DATES

Place each of these European champions next to the year they made their international debut from a choice of: **2018, 2016, 2010 ,2004, 2000, 2009**.

Giorgio Chiellini
Italy

Renato Sanches
Portugal

Sergio Busquets
Spain

Federico Chiesa
Italy

Rui Patrício
Portugal

Carles Puyol
Spain

Answers on page 64.

PLAYERS TO WATCH:
DEFENDERS

Playing in front of the keeper, a defender's first job is to stop the opposition scoring. As well as being strong and ready to tackle and block, top defenders in today's high-press era are also good passers and join in with attacks.

JOŠKO GVARDIOL

Country: **Croatia**
Club: **Manchester City**
Born: **23 January 2002**
Major honours: **FIFA World Cup 2022 third place**

A prized left-footed centre-back, Gvardiol is keen to build on his performances at UEFA EURO 2020. His all-round defensive game has gone from strength to strength in recent seasons, to the point where Gvardiol is seen as one of Europe's top defenders. He is quick, strong and very difficult to beat in the air.

MANUEL AKANJI

Country: **Switzerland**
Club: **Manchester City**
Born: **19 July 1995**
Major honours: **UEFA Champions League (x1), Premier League (x1)**

Switzerland's Akanji has taken his incredible club form with Manchester City onto the international stage. He is a defender able to play with both feet, comfortable in several positions and can carry the ball forward from his own half. After so much success in domestic football, Akanji is looking to take Switzerland deep into this tournament.

VIRGIL VAN DIJK

Country: **Netherlands**
Club: **Liverpool**
Born: **8 July 1991**
Major honours: **UEFA Champions League (x1), UEFA Super Cup (x1), Premier League (x1)**

The Netherlands' inspirational captain gives his nation a solid defensive base to build patient attacks from. Van Dijk's strength, speed and ability to win possession without risking clumsy fouls makes him a mighty obstacle for any attacking oppposition. If the Dutch want to go deep into this tournament, Van Dijk will be a key player.

ANDREAS CHRISTENSEN

Country: **Denmark**
Club: **Barcelona**
Born: **10 April 1996**
Major honours: **UEFA Champions League (x1), UEFA Europa League 2019, La Liga (x1)**

Christensen has excelled playing club football in both Spain and England, which has no doubt helped his Denmark form. Playing alongside captain Simon Kjær, the tall and athletic centre-back knows exactly when to tackle and press the opposition, and when to drop back and protect the area around his goal. He featured in all six games as Denmark reached the semi-finals at EURO 2020.

DANI CARVAJAL

Country: **Spain**
Club: **Real Madrid**
Born: **11 January 1992**
Major honours: **UEFA Nations League 2023, UEFA Champions League (x5), UEFA Super Cup (x4), La Liga (x3)**

Just like Jordi Alba at left-back, Carvajal is a vastly experienced full-back who uses his game knowledge, leadership and tenacious style to propel Spain to victory. From his usual right-back slot he gives his opposing winger very little space and time on the ball. Carvajal enjoys pushing forward from his own half and overlapping the midfielder in front of him.

JOHN STONES

Country: **England**
Club: **Manchester City**
Born: **28 May 1994**
Major honours: **UEFA EURO 2020 runner-up**, **UEFA Champions League (x1), Premier League (x5)**

Stones has forged a reputation as a centre-back that thrives on shutting down attacks and keeping clean sheets for England. He has also operated as a defensive midfielder for Manchester City and coach Gareth Southgate wants him to bring the ball out from defence whenever possible. Experienced and reliable, every team in the tournament would love to have him.

RÚBEN DIAS

Country: **Portugal**
Club: **Manchester City**
Born: **14 May 1997**
Major honours: **UEFA Nations League 2019, UEFA Champions League (x1), Premier League (x3)**

Whether Portugal play with a back three or four, Dias always shines and uses his immense defensive skills to keep even the best strikers quiet. His clever interceptions, blocks and tackles protect the goalkeeper, and he is also a thwarting presence when free-kicks and corners are launched into his box. Dias has the ability to stay focused even in high-pressure moments.

ANTONIO RÜDIGER

Country: **Germany**
Club: **Real Madrid**
Born: **3 March 1993**
Major honours: **UEFA Champions League (x1), UEFA Europa League (x1), UEFA Super Cup (x2), FIFA Club World Cup (x2)**

In one-on-one tackling, defending a crowded penalty area or pressing forward to win possession, Rüdiger is one of the best in the business. Quick over short and long distances, and with the strength to hold off most strikers, he creates a defensive wall that is so difficult to break down. Rüdiger is aggressive and combative but always in a controlled manner.

WILLIAM SALIBA

Country: **France**
Club: **Arsenal**
Born: **24 March 2001**
Major honours: **FIFA World Cup 2018 runner-up**

France legend Raphaël Varane retired in 2023, but there was no panic because William Saliba was the perfect defender to take over from him. Saliba has enjoyed a rapid rise through the international ranks and impressed coaches with his maturity and ability to excel in different tactical situations. His prime attributes are his speed and athleticism.

ANDREW ROBERTSON

Country: **Scotland**
Club: **Liverpool**
Born: **11 March 1994**
Major honours: **UEFA Champions League (x1), UEFA Super Cup (x1), Premier League (x1)**

Robertson is a left-back or wing-back who gives Scotland a brilliant forward outlet on top of his resolute defending. The captain leads by example and works super hard, covering many kilometres and frequently bursting down the wing to provide width and help to outnumber the opposition in attack. Robertson is aiming to take Scotland beyond the group stage.

PLAYERS TO WATCH:
GOALKEEPERS

Goalkeepers must be focused and alert for the entire match, because their split-second heroics can be the difference between a victory and defeat. This selection features the pick of the best.

UNAI SIMÓN

Country: **Spain**
Club: **Athletic Club**
Born: **11 June 1997**
Major honours: **UEFA Nations League 2023**

If Spain concede a penalty at this championship, or face sudden death penalties in a knockout game, Unai Simón is a fantastic goalkeeper to have. He saved spot kicks at UEFA EURO 2020, the 2022 FIFA World Cup and was a penalty-saving hero as Spain won the UEFA Nations League. Simón's high all-round abilities make him world class.

JAN OBLAK

Country: **Slovenia**
Club: **Atlético de Madrid**
Born: **7 January 1993**
Major honours: **UEFA Europa League (x1), UEFA Super Cup (x1), La Liga (x1)**

When Slovenia start their EURO 2024 campaign on 16 June, they have Oblak to thank for the huge role he played in the country's successful qualification. The captain kept a clean sheet in four of his eight qualifying games and with him between the posts, Denmark, Serbia and England will face a formidable barrier in Group C.

KASPER SCHMEICHEL

Country: **Denmark**
Club: **Anderlecht**
Born: **5 November 1986**
Major honours: **Premier League (x1), FA Cup (x1)**

Schmeichel's displays were first class when Denmark reached the semi-finals of UEFA EURO 2020. The awesome goalkeeper has his sights set on another great run at this tournament. Schmeichel commands his area with authority and his assured handling skills and acrobatic saves repel many attacks. EURO 2024 could be his final appearance at a major international event.

MARC-ANDRÉ TER STEGEN

Country: **Germany**
Club: **Barcelona**
Born: **30 April 1992**
Major honours: **UEFA Champions League (x1), UEFA Super Cup (x1), La Liga (x5)**

Ter Stegen's rivalry with the great Manuel Neuer to play for Germany has inspired both goalkeepers to continually excel. The Barcelona man is so difficult to beat in one-on-one situations and he's known to routinely pull out top-class saves. Ter Stegen's ability with his gloves and boots make him a titanic figure between the posts.

GIANLUIGI DONNARUMMA

Country: **Italy**
Club: **Paris Saint-Germain**
Born: **25 February 1999**
Major honours: **UEFA EURO 2020, UEFA Nations League third place 2021, 2023, Ligue 1 (x2)**

Crowned Player of the Tournament when Italy triumphed at UEFA EURO 2020, Donnarumma gives his country a brilliant defensive base and the platform to be victorious. Great at anticipating any attacking threats, he dominates his area with his size and judges perfectly when to race forward to intercept, or spring through the air to punch clear or push the ball wide.

PLAY-OFFS TO THE FINALS

Twenty of the teams at UEFA EURO 2024 were decided through the regular qualifying groups. Joining these and hosts Germany are the three victorious teams from the exciting play-offs. This play-off system was first used to determine the remaining teams taking part in EURO 2020.

In total, 12 teams competed in the play-offs on 21 and 26 March 2024. Participation was based on the teams' ranking in the 2022/23 UEFA Nations League and they were drawn into three paths of four teams. Two semi-finals and a final were played in each path to give three eventual winners. Go to EURO2024.com to discover the play-off results and fill in the scores and winners on the next page.

PATH A

Semi-final 1

Team:	v	Team:

Semi-final 2

Team:	v	Team:

Final

Winner 1:	v	Winner 2:

Play-off winner:

PATH B

Semi-final 1

Team:	v	Team:

Semi-final 2

Team:	v	Team:

Final

Winner 1:	v	Winner 2:

Play-off winner:

PATH C

Semi-final 1

Team:	v	Team:

Semi-final 2

Team:	v	Team:

Final

Winner 1:	v	Winner 2:

Play-off winner:

RECORD ALL THE ACTION

Catch all the games, goals and results from UEFA EURO 2024 and make sure you fill in the winners and all your favourite bits. It is the perfect place to record the mega moments from Europe's biggest football event!

UEFA EURO 2024 winners:

Runners-up:

Top Scorer:

He scored _____ goals.

Favourite team:

Favourite player:

He was the best because:

Favourite young player:

Most skilful player:

Best team to watch:

MY TEAM OF THE TOURNAMENT

GOALKEEPER

CENTRE-BACK

CENTRE-BACK

RIGHT-BACK

LEFT-BACK

MIDFIELDER

MIDFIELDER

MIDFIELDER

FORWARD

FORWARD

FORWARD

My favourite goal:

My favourite captain:

My favourite coach:

FIXTURES AND RESULTS

Who will lift the Henri Delauney Cup on 14 July in Berlin? Use the fill-in charts to follow every team's progress through the competition.

THE GROUP STAGE

Group A table

Team	P	W	D	L	GF	GA	Pts
1							
2							
3							
4							

Group B table

Team	P	W	D	L	GF	GA	Pts
1							
2							
3							
4							

Group C table

Team	P	W	D	L	GF	GA	Pts
1							
2							
3							
4							

Group D table

Team	P	W	D	L	GF	GA	Pts
1							
2							
3							
4							

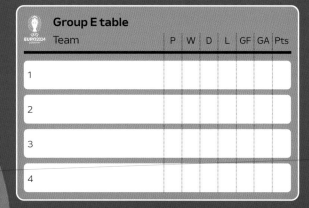

Group E table

Team	P	W	D	L	GF	GA	Pts
1							
2							
3							
4							

Group F table

Team	P	W	D	L	GF	GA	Pts
1							
2							
3							
4							

ROUND OF 16

Match 37, Dortmund — Winner Group A — Runner-up Group C
29 June

v

Goalscorers

Match 38, Berlin — Runner-up Group A — Runner-up Group B
29 June

v

Goalscorers

Match 39, Cologne — Winner Group B — Third place Group A/D/E/F
30 June

v

Goalscorers

Match 40, Gelsenkirchen — Winner Group C — Third place Group D/E/F
30 June

v

Goalscorers

Match 41, Frankfurt — Winner Group F — Third place Group A/B/C
1 July

v

Goalscorers

Match 42, Düsseldorf — Runner-up Group D — Runner-up Group E
1 July

v

Goalscorers

Match 43, Munich — Winner Group E — Third Group A/B/C/D
2 July

v

Goalscorers

Match 44, Leipzig — Winner Group D — Runner-up Group F
2 July

v

Goalscorers

QUARTER-FINALS

Match 45, Stuttgart Winner Match 39 Winner Match 37

5 July ◯ v ◯

Goalscorers

Match 46, Hamburg Winner Match 41 Winner Match 42

5 July ◯ v ◯

Goalscorers

Match 47, Berlin Winner Match 43 Winner Match 44

6 July ◯ v ◯

Goalscorers

Match 48 Düsseldorf Winner Match 40 Winner Match 38

6 July ◯ v ◯

Goalscorers

SEMI-FINALS

Match 49, Munich

Winner Match 45 | Winner Match 46

9 July | v | 21:00 (CET)

Goalscorers

Best moment of the match

Match 50, Dortmund

Winner Match 47 | Winner Match 48

10 July | v | 21:00 (CET)

Goalscorers

Best moment of the match

Match 51, Berlin   Winner Match 49   Winner Match 50

14 July   ⬤ v ⬤   21:00 (CET)

Line-ups

Substitutes

Goalscorers

Cards

Player of the Match

Best moment of the match

ANSWERS

Pages 32-33
TOP TENS
1. Zidane, 2. Xhaka, 3. Rooney, 4. Hazard, 5. Depay,
6. Modrić, 7. Costa, 8. Fàbregas, 9. Podolski,
10. Ibrahimović
TEN TESTS
1. False, 2. True, 3. True, 4. False, 5. True, 6. True, 7. True,
8. False, 9. False, 10. True.

Pages 34-35
SPOT THE DIFFERENCE

PAY THE PENALTY

B

C

Pages 36-37
KIT CLOSE-UP
1. Germany, 2. Ukraine, 3. Croatia, 4. Belgium,
5. Romania, 6. Spain.
TRAIN GAME
A. Ousmane Dembele, B. Jude Bellingham,
C. Leroy Sané

Pages 38-39
GOAL COUNT
Antoine Griezmann 7, Cristiano Ronaldo 14,
Michel Platini 9, David Villa 4 , Marco van Basten 5,
Patrick Kluivert 6
GOAL SCRAMBLE
1. Bukayo Saka, 2. Rasmus Højlund, 3. Scott McTominay,
4. Robert Lewandowski, 65. Rafael Leão, 6. Erling Haaland

Pages 40-41
NUMBER CRUNCH
Germany, Portugal, Scotland.
DIGIT DISPLAY
A 1964, B 19, C 60, D 196, E 14.

Pages 42-43
CHAMPIONS SEARCH

U	L	V	X	J	V	I	E	I	R	A	T	Z	G
W	F	D	O	S	O	C	A	S	I	L	L	A	S
O	S	Y	R	C	N	R	O	U	Q	J	X	G	F
N	W	M	U	G	X	K	G	C	C	G	V	O	C
T	A	L	O	N	S	O	Q	I	L	T	N	R	H
E	V	D	A	E	H	Y	S	K	N	I	E	A	I
C	C	E	E	X	S	I	L	V	A	H	C	K	E
T	A	X	R	S	U	K	K	G	J	F	O	I	L
S	X	R	I	R	C	P	D	M	U	V	L	S	L
H	E	I	V	X	A	H	E	Y	E	L	C	L	I
Q	S	N	B	A	U	T	A	P	W	D	L	T	N
C	B	J	K	S	L	K	T	M	E	M	E	I	I
I	J	K	P	H	D	H	X	I	P	D	H	R	T
X	A	V	I	R	A	M	O	S	L	S	V	R	P

WORD FIT

1. MUNICH
2. VAR
3. DEFENDER
4. THREE LIONS
5. REDS

(down) 6. CUTMEG, 7. HEADER, REFEREE, NETHERLANDS

Pages 44-45
HIT OR MISS?
Romelu Lukaku – hit, Raheem Sterling – miss, Diogo
Jota – hit, Álvaro Morata – miss, Ivan Perišić – hit, Kai
Havertz – hit.

Pages 46-47
FLASHBACK
1: 2016, **2**: 2012, **3**: 2008, **4**: 2020, **5**: 2004.
HOST PARTY
France – 2016, Sweden – 1992, Italy – 1980
BIRTHDAY BOYS
1994
DEBUT DATES
Giorgio Chiellini – 2004, Federico Chiesa – 2018,
Renato Sanches – 2016, Rui Patrício– 2010,
Sergio Busquets – 2009, Carles Puyol – 2000.